Soil

by Melissa Stewart

Heinemann Library
CHICAGO, ILLINOIS

Designed by Ox and Company

An Editorial Directions book

Printed in China

06 05 04
10 9 8 7 6 5

Library of Congress Cataloging-in-Publication Data
Stewart, Melissa.
    Soil / Melissa Stewart.
        p. cm.—(Rocks and minerals)
Includes bibliographical references and index.
Summary: Provides an overview of soil, discussing its formation, composition, and uses.
    ISBN: 1-58810-260-2 (HC), 1-4034-0096-2 (Pbk.)
    1. Soils—Juvenile literature. 2. Soil ecology—Juvenile literature. [1. Soils.
    2. Soil ecology. 3. Ecology.] I. Title.
    S591.3 .S73 2002
    631.4—dc21   2001002761

Acknowledgments
The author and publishers are grateful to the following for permission to reproduce copyright material:

Photographs ©: Cover background, Corbis; cover foreground, E. Webber/Visuals Unlimited, Inc.; p. 4 Bob Daemmrich/The
Image Works; p. 5 Dr. Jeremy Burgess/Science Photo Library/Photo Researchers, Inc.; p. 6 John Gerlach/Visuals Unlimited,
Inc.; p. 7 Don W. Fawcett/Visuals Unlimited, Inc.; p. 8 Grace Davies Photography; p. 9 Corbis; p. 11 Glenn M. Oliver/Visuals
Unlimited, Inc.; p. 12 Bea Hunn/Visuals Unlimited, Inc.; p. 13 John Sohlden/Visuals Unlimited, Inc.; p. 14 James P. Rowan;
p. 15 Paul Kern/Bettmann/Corbis; p. 16 Bettmann/Corbis; p. 17 Townsend P. Dickinson/The Image Works; p.18 James P.
Rowan; p. 19 John Holmes/Frank Lane Picture Agency/Corbis; p. 20 Tom Bean; p. 21 Townsend P. Dickinson/The Image
Works; p. 22 top Cameramann International, Ltd.; p. 22 bottom Grace Davies Photography; p. 24 Bettmann/Corbis; p. 25 Bill
Everitt/Tom Stack & Associates; p. 26 Buddy Mays/Corbis; p. 27 Grace Davies Photography; p. 28 J. Lotter/Tom Stack &
Associates; p. 29 Grace Davies Photography.

Every effort has been made to contact copyright holders of any material reproduced in this book. Any omissions will be rectified
in subsequent printings if notice is given to the publisher.

Some words are shown in bold, **like this.** You can find out what they mean by looking in the glossary.

Contents

What Is Soil?

If you go outside and dig up a small patch of grass, what do you think you will see underneath? You will see dirt, or soil, of course. Maybe you've wondered whether dirt and soil are exactly the same. Actually, there is a difference.

The word "soil" is used only to describe the material that covers Earth's surface. The word "dirt" can be used to describe soil or anything that is not clean. Animal waste is sometimes called dirt, and so is dust. Dust is a mixture of soil particles, hair strands, insect parts, food crumbs, and other things.

This girl is taking a look at the soil in her backyard. It is a good place to grow flowers and vegetables.

DIRT FOR DINNER?

For thousands of years, certain groups of people have eaten soil. They think it can bring good luck. Scientists admit that soil can provide **nutrients** that some people may not get from the foods they eat. But that's no reason to scoop up a handful of soil and pop it into your mouth. Eating soil could make you very sick—it could even kill you!

You've probably seen it lots of times, but did you ever take a really close look at soil? Did you ever wonder what it is made of? Soil is made of broken-up rocks, water, air, and bits of rotting material. An average soil sample is about 45 percent broken-up rocks, 25 percent water, 25 percent air, and 5 percent rotting material.

Where does the rotting material come from? When leaves and twigs fall to the ground, they slowly rot, or decay, and become part of the soil. Animal waste gradually breaks down and becomes part of the soil, too. All living things become part of the soil when they die.

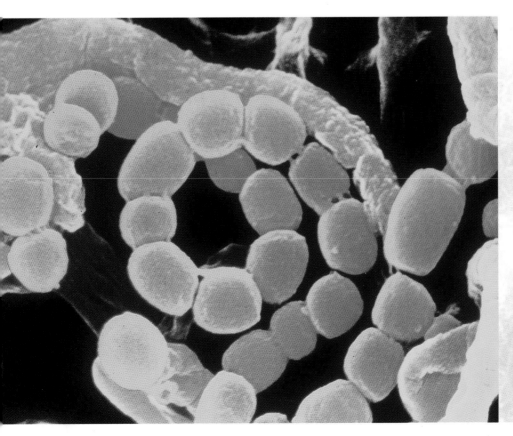

DID YOU KNOW?

Soil provides a good meal and a safe home for many living things. Some of these creatures are so small that you need a microscope to see them (such as the soil **bacterium** at left). Believe it or not, there can be more of these tiny creatures in one spoonful of soil than the number of people living on Earth—billions!

How Soil Forms

All soil begins as solid rock. Rock forms slowly over millions of years. Even though it may seem very tough, rock is not indestructible. As soon as it forms, natural forces begin to break it apart. Over time, giant boulders gradually become small stones, then gravel, then pebbles, and then sand or even smaller particles. When these tiny bits of rock mix with other materials, new soil is created.

Crashing ocean waves, spreading glaciers, whipping winds, and other natural forces slowly **erode,** or wear away, rock on Earth's surface. Rocks may also break up by bumping into one another as fast-flowing streams carry them to the ocean. Rock deep underground can be

Waves and water currents slowly erode Lake Superior's rocky shore. Over time, giant boulders break down and form the lake's sandy bottom.

DID YOU KNOW?

Soil forms slowly, but it can be destroyed quickly. It can take more than 500 years to form 1 inch (2.5 centimeters) of soil, but a ferocious storm can wash away that soil in just a few minutes. Farmers know erosion can do a lot of damage to their fields, so they plant different plants in the same place in different years. This process is called crop rotation.

eroded by seeping rainwater. Even Earth's tallest mountains are affected by the power of erosion.

A process called **weathering** can also break down rock. Sometimes, plant roots grow into a rock's cracks, pushing against the rock and eventually splitting it. Repeated freezing and thawing can cause a rock to shrink and expand. Over time, this process may weaken a rock and cause it to crumble into bits.

Wind and sand have eroded these large rocks in Wyoming. Weathering has caused visible cracks.

Soil Covers Earth

A handful of soil reveals many things: bits of rock, plant roots, rotting materials, and tiny creatures. The color and texture tell you what type of soil it is.

Soil covers most of Earth's surface. It lies under lush forests and dry deserts, tall buildings and winding roads, and even at the bottom of the oceans. The only places without soil are the tops of tall mountains and places so cold that they are made of solid ice.

In some areas, the soil is a few inches thick. In others, it can be several feet deep. The amount of soil in an area depends

DID YOU KNOW?

The deep ocean is a cold, dark place. Few creatures can survive in such a harsh environment. The soil along the ocean floor builds up slowly over time. It is littered with millions of tiny skeletons of animals that once lived closer to the water's surface. These skeletons take much longer to break down than dead material on land.

on the weather and the mixture of materials nearby.

Some of the richest soils in the world are found near volcanoes. When a volcano erupts, it often releases huge quantities of ash and dust particles. These materials contain a variety of **nutrients** that help plants live and grow.

We could not live without soil. The plants that grow in soil give us the food we eat and the oxygen we breathe. Rice, the most important crop in the world, grows in fields of wet soil called paddies. Lettuce, tomatoes, oranges, corn, grapes, carrots, and peas grow on large farms and in small gardens all over the world.

Plants also provide us with shade on hot summer days and give us fuel to heat our homes during long, cold winters. Some important medicines come from plants that grow in tropical rain forest soils. The cotton in your T-shirts grows on large farms in warm parts of the world. The paper in this book was probably made from trees that grow in northern forests.

OUR PRECIOUS PLANET

On April 22 each year, people around the world celebrate Earth Day. It is a time to remember how special our planet is and to think of ways to protect important **natural resources,** such as soil.

New plants are beginning to grow in this California field. Much of California's richest soil is composed of materials that wash down from nearby mountains.

Layers of Soil

ON THE LOOKOUT

You may be able to see layers of soil without digging down into the ground. The next time you take a walk in a natural area, look for **eroded** stream banks. Can you spot the different layers?

If you dig down into the ground, you will notice that the soil begins to change as you go deeper. Near the surface, the soil is dark brown and loosely packed, with very few large rocks. Deeper down, the soil has a lighter color, is more tightly packed, and is full of rocks. The soil is different because it forms in layers. The soil in the upper layers is older and contains more materials than the soil in the lower layers.

The first few inches of soil are called **topsoil.** Topsoil is usually dark brown and has plenty of rotting material and tiny creatures mixed in. The roots of most plants are found in this layer. All

Soil is constantly being created. How the different layers of soil develop depends on the parent material, creatures in the soil, surface features, climate, and time.

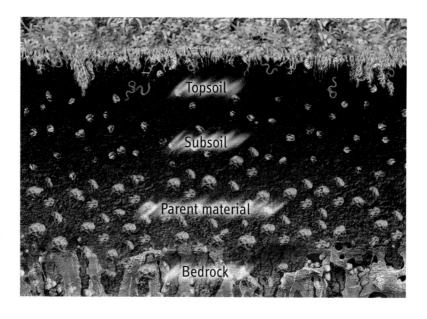

Topsoil

Subsoil

Parent material

Bedrock

the materials in topsoil help to keep it loosely packed with plenty of air pockets. When you rub topsoil between your fingers, it feels soft and slightly spongy.

Below the topsoil is a layer called the **subsoil.** Subsoil is usually light brown. It has more rock and less rotting material than topsoil. It also has fewer spaces for air and water. When you rub subsoil between your fingers, it feels a bit gritty.

The **parent material** lies below the subsoil. It has no rotting material at all and is more tightly packed than the layers above it. The parent material may be gray or yellowish brown. It is usually made up of clay and sand with chunks of rock and gravel. The rocks and gravel have chipped off the solid **bedrock** below the parent material. New soil begins to form in this layer.

Three Kinds of Soil

This sunny beach is covered with countless pieces of tiny soil particles called sand. Most plants do not grow well in sandy soil, but certain grassy species can survive.

The bits of rock that make up soil come in three sizes—large, medium, and small. The largest bits are called sand. You can see plenty of sand if you go to the beach. The medium-size bits are called silt. Silt is just large enough to see. The smallest bits are called clay. You need a microscope to see grains of clay. Sand, silt, and clay are the three kinds of soil.

Most plants do not grow well in soil that has a lot of sand. Rainwater drains through sand so quickly that plants dry up. Desert soil is very sandy, but cactuses can still grow in deserts because they have special ways to hold onto water. Their spiny leaves lose less water to **evaporation** than do the broad leaves of plants in fields and forests. Also, cactus stems can store large quantities of water, and their roots fan out in every direction. A saguaro cactus's roots may be more than 75 feet (23 meters) long.

DID YOU KNOW?

In the late 1880s, the Denver and Rio Grande Western Railroad gave the name Silt to a town in western Colorado. The town was named for the soil in the area because the silt made it difficult to lay tracks.

The stems of the rare organ pipe cactus can hold many gallons of water. It grows only in the Sonoran Desert of Arizona and Mexico.

Soils that contain more silt and clay are better for growing plants because these soils hold more rainwater. They usually have more rotting material, too. But soil that has no sand in it may drain so slowly that plant roots start to rot. Plants grow best in soils with plenty of rotting material and equal parts of sand, silt, and clay. This kind of soil is called loam.

WHAT KIND OF SOIL DO YOU HAVE?

SOIL TYPE	WHEN DRY SOIL IS SQUEEZED	WHEN WET SOIL IS SQUEEZED
Sand	Feels gritty, falls apart	Holds together, but crumbles easily
Silt	Feels smooth and silky, holds together	Holds together and does not crumble easily, but cannot be rolled into a long, snake-shaped strand
Clay	Feels slippery or sticky, breaks into hard clumps	Holds together and can be rolled into a long, snake-shaped strand

A Look at Humus

The dense plant life in this forest provides rotting material for humus. In turn, the humus supplies the plants with important nutrients.

Farmers and scientists use the word **humus** to describe the bits of rotting material in the upper layers of soil. Humus is usually dark brown or black and is full of the **nutrients** that plants need to live and grow. Like glue, humus helps hold together the bits of rock in soil. Like a sponge, humus soaks up water and holds onto it.

DID YOU KNOW?

Farmers in North America's Great Plains grow rye, oats, and barley as well as wheat and corn. All these plants are kinds of grasses that grow well in the soil of that region.

The amount of humus in soil has a lot to do with the kinds of plants that grow in an area. The soil in forests usually has plenty of humus. As a result, many different kinds of trees, shrubs, and ground plants grow in most forests.

Grasslands also have rich soil. Natural grasslands support many kinds of grasses, some trees, and a rich variety of wildflowers. Prairie grasslands are also home to pronghorns, buffalo, prairie dogs, and many birds and insects. Lions, zebras, giraffes, and elephants live on savanna grasslands in Africa.

The Great Plains grasslands of North America have some of the best soil in the world. American and Canadian farmers harvest tons of corn and wheat in these areas every year. The corn is used to feed cattle and people. The wheat is used in many popular foods, including breakfast cereal, pasta, bread, cakes, and cookies.

Some swamps and most bogs have a kind of soil called peat. Peat contains more humus and less rocky material than other soils. It can hold a lot of water and is good for growing plants such as cranberries, peat moss, and Venus's-flytraps.

For many years, people thought swamps, marshes, and other wetlands were useless. Now we know that the soils and plants in wetlands can remove pollutants and other harmful chemicals from the water.

HOW PEOPLE USE PEAT

In some parts of the world, people burn peat to keep warm. Some people dig up the peat themselves, while others buy it at peat farms. Peat farmers also sell peat to plant nurseries and garden centers. When the humus-rich soil is added to other kinds of soils, plants thrive.

Tiny Soil Creatures

Most soil contains billions of creatures so small that you need a microscope to see them. These tiny living things belong to two groups—**bacteria** and **fungi.** Bacteria and fungi are not plants, but they are not animals either.

Bacteria are one-celled creatures that live for a few hours or a few days. They reproduce by splitting in half. Some bacteria cause deadly diseases, but most are harmless to humans. They can be found just

IMAGINE THAT!

No one knew that bacteria existed until the late 1600s when a Dutch cloth merchant named Anton van Leeuwenhoek (left) saw them in a simple microscope he had built. It took even longer for scientists to realize that some bacteria make people sick. They can cause tooth decay, strep throat, tonsillitis, scarlet fever, impetigo, and other illnesses. Today, doctors use drugs called antibiotics to kill the bacteria that make us sick.

about everywhere—in your house, in your body, in the ocean, and in the soil.

Fungi are living things belonging to a group that includes molds, yeasts, and other creatures. Most fungi live underground, so you never see them. But you may have seen mushrooms, puffballs, or stinkhorns in the woods. Their structures help the fungi reproduce, just as flowers help plants reproduce.

Bacteria and fungi have a very important job. They make **humus** by consuming tons of autumn leaves, the flesh of dead animals, and even each other. As these tiny creatures break down materials, they return **nutrients** to the soil.

Most fungi live underground. When conditions are right, some produce mushrooms that release spores, so more fungi can grow in new places.

Without bacteria and fungi, nothing on Earth would decay. Nutrients would never get back into the soil, and plants cannot grow in soil that has no nutrients. If there were no plants on Earth, animals—including humans—would have nothing to eat. Bacteria and fungi may be small, but they are an important part of every **ecosystem** in the world.

DID YOU KNOW?

In cold parts of the world, many of the tiny creatures that live in the soil become inactive during the winter.

Plants in the Soil

Grassland soils are rich in nutrients. They can support an abundance of plant life, such as the Blazing Star in this Illinois prairie.

Almost all plants need soil to grow. Most plants grow best in warm, moist soil that has plenty of **humus,** a variety of tiny living creatures, and a mixture of sand, silt, and clay. That is why more plants live in the world's forests, grasslands, and wetlands than in dry deserts or on the chilly **tundra** of the far North.

THAT'S INCREDIBLE!

Some plants do not grow in soil. They get all the nutrients they need from water and air. Duckweed and water hyacinths live in stagnant ponds and lakes. Their roots dangle a few inches below the water's surface, but they do not touch the bottom. Spanish moss and orchids are air plants. They hang from the branches of tall trees.

The humus and rocky materials in soil give plants all the **nutrients** they need to live, grow, and make flowers. Without energy from the Sun and nutrients from the soil, plants could not produce the leaves, nuts, and fruits that rabbits, cows, zebras, elephants, and many other animals eat. The meat eaters, such as wolves, lions, jaguars, eagles, and owls, hunt the plant eaters for food. As a result, meat-eating **predators** depend on plants, too. Plants are an important part of every **ecosystem** on Earth. Without soil to grow plants, many living things would not survive. Plants rob nutrients from the soil, but they also help the soil. The roots of plants in fields and forests grow down into the soil and help hold it together. As a result, less soil is **eroded** by the wind and rain. Plants that grow in wetlands prevent flooding and often remove dangerous poisons from the soil.

As plant roots grow downward, they sometimes force themselves into tiny cracks and crevices in rocks. Over time, the roots break up the rocks and help make new soil.

DID YOU KNOW?

The rafflesia plant of Malaysia (right) produces the largest flowers in the world. Like other plants, it could not produce such large blossoms if it did not get plenty of nutrients from the soil.

Animals in the Soil

Animals need soil to survive. The grass that horses, zebras, cattle, and sheep feed on grows in soil, as do the fruits and seeds that many birds eat. Without soil, there would be no brightly colored flowers with sugary nectar to feed busy bees, hovering hummingbirds, and fluttering butterflies.

Large groups of prairie dogs live together in communities called "towns." The animals in each town dig a huge network of underground tunnels in the soil.

The soil also provides a safe home for many kinds of animals. In some parts of the world, 1 acre (0.4 hectare) of soil can support five to ten tons of living creatures. Many slugs, beetles, flatworms, and millipedes spend their entire lives in soil. They find plenty of food there. Woodchucks, chipmunks, rabbits, skunks, and prairie dogs sleep and hide from enemies in underground burrows. Many other creatures spend the coldest months of winter **hibernating** in the soil.

Animals are also important to soil. Grazing animals leave manure behind. When **bacteria** and **fungi** break down the manure, they add a variety of **nutrients** to the soil. During the summer, mice, moles, and shrews plow through the soil in search of food. Beetles, centipedes, and earthworms also make trails through the soil. Air and water can fill the spaces these animals leave behind. Plant roots need plenty of fresh air and water.

INCREDIBLE EARTHWORMS

As earthworms wriggle through the soil, they suck up all the dirt in their path. In fact, a single earthworm "eats" several pounds of soil each year. The waste materials that earthworms leave behind are called "castings." Castings are full of nutrients. Scientist can tell how healthy the soil is by looking at the earthworms living in it. If the soil has too much water or too few nutrients, the earthworms look pale.

Nutrients in the Soil

This worker is spraying a cornfield with liquid fertilizer. While fertilizers provide crops with needed nutrients, they can also pollute groundwater.

Plants get the **nutrients** they need from the soil. Some nutrients come from **humus.** Others come from the **minerals** in rocky particles of sand, silt, and clay. Sometimes plants use up the nutrients in soil faster than new ones are created, so farmers often add fertilizers containing nitrogen and phosphorus to their fields.

Rabbits are plant eaters. They enjoy munching on a wide range of grasses.

When a plant-eating animal, such as a rabbit, chomps on grass, the nutrients in the plant enter the rabbit's body. The rabbit uses the nutrients to keep its heart, brain, and muscles working. When a meat eater, such as a fox, eats the rabbit, some of the nutrients become part of the fox's body.

22

It uses these important chemicals to make its own body function properly. When the fox dies, **bacteria** and **fungi** go to work on its carcass. In just a few weeks, they break down the **predator's** body, and the nutrients are returned to the soil. In this way, nutrients cycle through an **ecosystem.**

NUTRIENTS AND THE LIFE CYCLE

NUTRIENT	WHAT IT DOES FOR PLANTS	WHAT IT DOES FOR ANIMALS
Calcium	Helps plants take in other nutrients; helps roots and leaves grow	Helps animals make bones and teeth and keeps them strong
Magnesium	Helps plants use sunlight to make food	Helps animals keep their hearts and blood vessels healthy
Nitrogen	Helps plants grow and stay green	Not used by animals
Phosphorus	Helps plants make flowers, fruits, and seeds	Helps animals keep their brains and nerves working; helps break down vitamins
Potassium	Helps plants fight diseases	Helps animals keep their muscles strong and healthy; helps keep blood flowing

How People Use Soil

This Texas farm was deserted because all the **topsoil** eroded during the Dust Bowl of the 1930s. The plants farmers were trying to grow could not survive a period of massive droughts.

Of course you know that farmers grow wheat, corn, and vegetables in the soil. The plants farmers feed to cattle, pigs, and other animals also grow in soil. Farmers know it is important to keep the soil

FARMING IN DELTAS

A delta is a piece of land where a river deposits mud, sand, and gravel as it enters a larger body of water, such as an ocean. Deltas are often three-sided. In fact, the delta got its name from the Greek letter delta (Δ), because of its triangle shape. The soil in a delta is made of clay, sand, and silt. This soil is full of nutrients. All those nutrients make the delta soil an excellent

place for farming. For thousands of years, these fertile lands around the world have helped farmers grow many crops.

The Nile River in Egypt, the Brahmaputra and Ganges Rivers in India, and the Mississippi River in Louisiana have some of the world's largest deltas. In the Mississippi Delta, local farmers grow cotton, rice, and sugar cane.

rich. Many farmers add fertilizer and try to prevent the land from **eroding.** Some farmers also rotate their crops. Because different plants require different **nutrients,** rotating crops each year means the soil can grow healthy plants season after season.

People also use soil in other ways. Artists use clay to make pottery. Before they start shaping the clay, they dry it, crush it, and strain it. This gets rid of unwanted materials in the clay. When artists finish sculpting a vase or a bowl, they bake it at a high temperature in an oven called a kiln.

Sand can be used to make glass and explosives and to filter water. It is also an important ingredient in many building materials, including cement, concrete, mortar, and plaster. Some people use adobe to build houses. Adobe, a mixture of soil, straw, and water, is poured into molds and dried to make bricks. Most adobe houses are coated with plaster to keep the adobe dry.

Native Americans in Taos, New Mexico, built this adobe pueblo, or dwelling, about 800 years ago. Adobe falls apart if it gets wet, so builders can use it only in areas with low rainfall.

Studying Soil

A sieve can help you separate the materials in soil. You can make your own sieve by putting fine wire mesh in a frame or box.

Now that you know how very important soil is, maybe it's time to take a closer look. When you see soil from a distance, it may seem like nothing more than a dark brown, lumpy material. But soil is more interesting than you might think. Have you ever run your fingers through soil to see how it feels? Have you ever smelled soil? If not, it's time to give it a try.

Grab a shovel and head out to your backyard or a local park. Dig up some dirt and spread it out on a newspaper. You may want to use a **sieve** to separate the materials that make up the soil. Look at the soil closely with a hand lens. You will see some pebbles and tiny bits of rock.

DID YOU KNOW?

Ped is the Latin word for "foot," so you could think of pedologists as scientists who study the material found beneath our feet.

26

You may also see pieces of rotting plants. Do you see any insects or earthworms? What else is in your soil sample? In your notebook, be sure to write down everything you observe.

Now go to another spot and dig up some soil there. Compare the two samples. When you have studied both soil samples, return the soil to the ground, put your tools away, and wash your hands thoroughly.

Some scientists spend many hours studying and classifying soil. They note where the soil was found and the amount and type of materials in it. These scientists are called **pedologists.** Pedologists can help farmers decide what crops they should grow in the soil. They can also help make soil just right for growing a particular kind of plant.

PUTTING SCIENCE TO WORK

For many years, soil engineers in Pisa, Italy, have been studying the layers of topsoil and subsoil around the Leaning Tower of Pisa (above). They have now taken steps to stabilize the tower so that it does not tip any further.

Sources of Soil

This woman is inspecting young fir trees. Soon they will be planted in a forest area as part of a reforestation effort.

Soil is a **natural resource.** Wood, iron, and oil are also natural resources. We use all these materials to make important products. We make houses, furniture, and paper from wood. Iron is the main ingredient in steel, used in making cars, tractors, machinery, and skyscrapers. Oil keeps our houses warm in winter. It is also an important ingredient in plastics and in the gasoline that keeps our cars running.

Iron and oil are nonrenewable natural resources. Once we use up nonrenewable resources, we cannot replace them. But trees are a renewable natural resource, and so is soil. It takes many years for trees to grow, but if we replant them carefully, we

SEE FOR YOURSELF

If you have a yard, you might want to try making compost. Begin by buying a compost container—or use a wooden box about the size of a trash can. Put the container in a shady corner of your yard. Every time you mow the lawn, rake leaves, or peel a vegetable, add the left-over plant materials to your container. Always be sure to wash your hands thoroughly as soon as you go back into the house.

Over time, the plants will rot and compost will form. It will take at least a year to make your first batch of compost, so be patient. To speed things up, you can wet the pile with a hose and turn the materials over with a shovel about once a month.

will never run out of trees. People can also create more soil—but it takes quite a bit of time and effort. People need to be careful not to use up trees and soil faster than they can be replaced.

You may know someone who makes his or her own soil. Many people who like to grow flowers or vegetables make **compost** for their gardens. Instead of throwing away plant materials, they use them to create compost. Compost is a dark, crumbly mixture of rotting plant material. Unlike **humus,** it does not contain the remains of animals. Compost may include fallen leaves, grass clippings, and vegetable and fruit scraps from the kitchen. As compost forms, the **nutrients** from the plants break down. When compost is mixed with soil, new plants can absorb those nutrients, helping them to grow better.

Starting a backyard compost pile is a great idea. With a little patience, you can turn kitchen scraps and colorful autumn leaves into a nutrient-rich material that will help plants grow.

Glossary

bacterium: tiny living thing that may feed on rotting material. The plural of bacterium is bacteria. Some bacteria carry diseases that make people sick.

bedrock: layer of solid rock just below the soil

compost: mixture of rotting plant material that adds nutrients to soil

ecosystem: community of living things and their environment

erode: to slowly wear away over time by the action of wind, water, or glaciers

evaporation: process that changes a liquid into a gas

friction: force that resists motion between two objects or surfaces

fungus: living thing that is neither a plant nor an animal. The plural of fungus is fungi.

hibernating: resting or sleeping for the winter

humus: rotting material in soil

mineral: natural solid material with a specific chemical makeup and structure

natural resource: natural material that humans use to make important products

nutrient: natural chemical that plants and animals need for their bodies to work properly

parent material: bottom layer of soil. It contains large pieces of gravel and rock, but no humus.

pedologist: scientist who studies and classifies soil based on where it is found and the amount and type of materials in it

predator: animal that hunts and kills other animals for food

sieve: strainer, or filter, used to separate tiny pieces from large ones

subsoil: middle layer of soil. It contains larger pieces of rock and less humus than topsoil.

topsoil: top layer of soil. It contains small bits or rock and large quantities of rotting material.

tundra: ecosystem in the far North where summer is very short and only a few kinds of plants and animals can survive

weathering: breaking down of rock by plant roots or by repeated freezing and thawing

To Find Out More

BOOKS

Bial, Raymond. *A Handful of Dirt*. New York: Walker, 2000.

Bocknek, Jonathan. *The Science of Soil*. Milwaukee, Wis.: Gareth Stevens, 1999.

Burnett, Frances Hodgson. *The Secret Garden*. New York: Bantam Classics, 1987.

Lavies, Bianca. *Compost Critters*. New York: Dutton, 1993.

Sneeden, Robert. *Rocks and Soil*. Austin, Tex.: Raintree/Steck-Vaughn, 1998.

ORGANIZATIONS

International Erosion Control Association
P.O. Box 774904
1355 S. Lincoln Avenue
Steamboat Springs, CO 80477
907/879-3010

Soil and Water Conservation Society
7515 N.E. Ankeny Road
Ankeny, IA 50021
515/289-2331

Index

BATTLESHIP ARIZONA

An Illustrated History

Paul Stillwell

NAVAL INSTITUTE PRESS
ANNAPOLIS, MARYLAND

The drawings on pp. 261–65 are © 1991 by John F. De Virgilio.

The drawings on pp. 282–85 are © 1990 by Jerry L. Livingston.

The drawings on pp. 362–75 are © 1991 by Alan B. Chesley.

Library of Congress Cataloging-in-Publication Data

Stillwell, Paul, 1944–
    Battleship Arizona: an illustrated history / Paul Stillwell.
        p.   cm.
    Includes bibliographical references and index.
    ISBN 0-87021-023-8
    1. Arizona (Battleship)—History.   2. Pearl Harbor (Hawaii),
Attack on, 1941.   I. Title.
VA65.A6S75   1991
359.3′252′0973—dc20   91-14519

Printed in the United States of America on acid-free paper ∞

9 8 7 6 5 4 3 2

First printing

Title-page photo: The *Arizona* at full-dress ship for a holiday in the early 1930s. (Sunset Photo, Inc., courtesy Mrs. Jean Hatton)